3071

Music Minus One Piano

Mozart

Piano Quintet in Eb Major, K.452

Piano Quintet in Eb Major, K.452

4 taps (1 measure) precede music.

(A)

3071

4

21 **Allegro moderato.**

Allegro moderato. ⁴taps (1 measure) precede music.

26 **(C)**

3071

5

3071

6

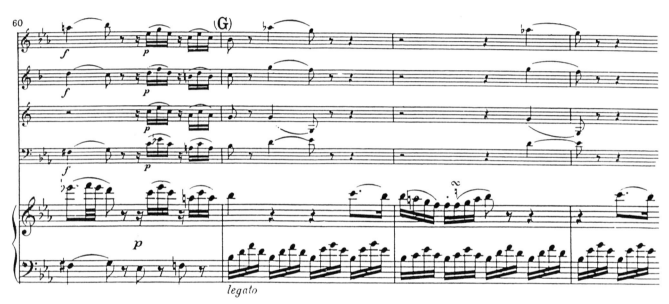

3071

3071

120

Larghetto

Larghetto

9

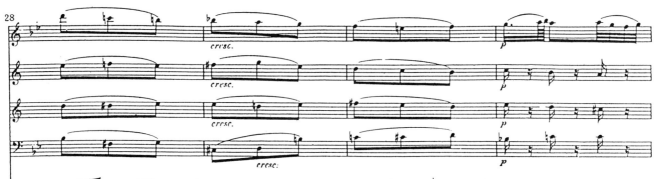

118

RONDO
Allegretto

Allegretto   3 taps precede music. / 1 2 / 1 begin /

10

(A)

legato

3071

110

115

120

Cadenza in tempo.

Cadenza in tempo.

(F)

3071

COMPACT DISC PAGE AND BAND INFORMATION

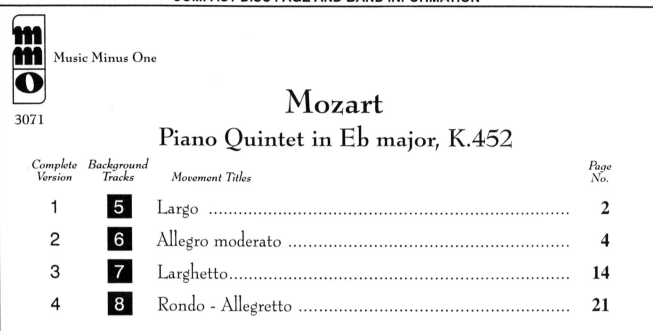

Music Minus One

3071

Mozart
Piano Quintet in Eb major, K.452

Complete Version	Background Tracks	Movement Titles	Page No.
1	5	Largo	2
2	6	Allegro moderato	4
3	7	Larghetto..	14
4	8	Rondo - Allegretto	21

Music Minus One • 50 Executive Boulevard • Elmsford, New York 10523-1325
Website: www.musicminusone.com   Phone: 914-592-1188 • Fax: 914-592-3575